Somewhere Beyond the Body

Somewhere Beyond the Body

Where Life Is Lived in Translucent Language

POEMS BY
T. P. BIRD

RESOURCE *Publications* • Eugene, Oregon

SOMEWHERE BEYOND THE BODY
Where Life Is Lived in Translucent Language

Resource Publications
An Imprint of Wipf and Stock Publishers
199 W. 8th Ave., Suite 3
Eugene, OR 97401

www.wipfandstock.com

PAPERBACK ISBN: 978-1-7252-9736-4
HARDCOVER ISBN: 978-1-7252-9737-1
EBOOK ISBN: 978-1-7252-9738-8

To my wife, Sally,
and our three daughters,
Elizabeth, Erin & Sarah

Contents

CONTENTS

PART THREE
The Life of Poetry

Contents

Part One

Life: A Small Inductive Study

*"Induction: Method of reasoning
from particulars to generals;
the conclusion thus arrived at."*
—Webster's Expanded
Dictionary (1993)

*"Here we encounter the general
difficulty of all interpretations.
The whole of the work must be
understood from individual words
and their combinations, but full
understanding of an individual part
presupposes understanding of the whole ...
Theoretically we are here at
the limits of all interpretation."*
—Wilhelm Dilthey (1833–1911)
'The development of Hermeneutics'

When

1.

When I was unborn a long time,
the world to me was yet unknown;
though dangerous—yet still with
beauty, it did not touch my body,
my soul, nor my orphaned spirit.
Its days, years and decades were
but words in a book not yet read,
or the stories not yet heard beneath
or between the hulking bodies of
those who came before.

2.

When I was newly born and then
long imprisoned in the silence of
my inner incubation—mysteries
and myths remained inaudible,
concealed like the lustful thoughts
of a billion good men.
Swaddled only in the blankets of
infancy and not in the knowledge
of an impending life, I had only
the comfort of my mother's arms.

3.

When dreams became remembered,
the world of my sleeping hours
invaded my subconscious. Thus,
I grew aware of life's dark shadows
that could loom over a toddler's bed
like a specter abusing my trust in abiding
love with terrifying dream images:
my mother turned devil-like in the night.
If my mind had allowed, I might have
grasped that I had come into this world
fully packaged with the dreadful
knowledge of both good *and* evil,
that my days would be filled with
awesome beauty—but also appalling,
buried fears.

4.

When long as an awakened child,
playing and learning, the world was
a theater of imagination—acts and
scenes coming in flashes of premonition
like wakening from one life into
another, as if stepping from a dark
room into daylight—my knowledge
of the cosmos limited to the thin,
broad sweep of innocence—
without the addition of subplots
and hoary agendas. Here I would
first hear the stories from beneath
and between the hulking bodies of

those who came before—many
staying hidden in the soft mist
of childhood memory.

5.

When long I was gripped in the
pathos of adolescence, the world
shrunk to the limits of self-awareness.
All I knew was the uncertainty of
my next breath, and the rawness
of my awkwardness. It did not matter
what I thought was real—the world
of beauty ignored my clumsy pleas.
And while a heavy universe leaned
on my thin and untrained shoulders—
my only reprieve were experiences
heard in the stories of those who
came before. These were my escape.

6.

When I passed into early adulthood—
an immature time slightly stranger
than memory, the world opened
its coat flaps to show me its secrets—
shiny bobbles and brilliant ideas
striking me like a blow from a
hammer. An ersatz wisdom spoke
to me through the lyrics of Dylan,
the vocal rhythms of Aretha, and
Clapton's lead guitar.
So much for the stories of old men;

I sat at the feet of youth-filled dreams,
where sex was the reward for resolve
in a world surely destined to change
for the good of all mankind.

7.
When in the long days from youth
to old age, my knowledge of the
world grew in length, if not in width
or depth, for narrow became the way
of *epignosis* in a world of swirling,
pathetic egos. I now sometimes
listen for the sound of my breathing,
but instead hear the wind rustling
dry leaves in spaces long abandoned.
Aging has become the awareness
of monthly magazine subscriptions
coming faster than ever before.

8.
When I have been dead a long time,
and have forgotten how to breath,
and the world has passed away into
ether, I'm assured "I will know as
I am known," for the end is just the
beginning of the stories told by the
souls within the brilliant bodies
of those who went before.

Where

1.
Where I am is the place in
the so-called present tense
of *when & where* I unfold like
a hand-written letter—sent
to myself—telling me of
the astonishing adventure
I'm having among the
goings-on of everyday life.

I must read the moment quickly,
for I find I'm finite, imperfect,
just a creature—not the Creator,
unable to stop time's forward
motion.
      I must read the faces,
the language of gesture,
the words spoken to me
and others with the speed of
thought in the present *when* &
where.
      And still . . . this is not
fast enough to keep the moment
from being lost in the steady
breeze that blows backwards
into *when* and *where . . .*

2.
I was . . . or at least a place
I thought I was—for it
resembles a place where
I might've been,
yet contradicts where
I thought I'd been. And so,
I unfold—again like a letter
addressed to myself—
but slowly, deliberately . . .

However, the ink has faded,
the paper terribly crinkled
with the mind's handling,
sentences half finished,
punctuation so badly done—
tis hard to discern
the specifics, the minutia,
the meaning behind the faces,
the gestures and the words
scrawled in such haste.
I'm many times more the finite,
imperfect creature—unable to
keep this time and place from
morphing, morphing, morphing
into mud.

3.

However, let this be clear:
the letter to myself that will
unfold in a distant place, in
the *whenever and wherever*
it might be—cannot be
written now in neither the
steady hand of death, nor
the spidery scrawl of very
old age, though both are
sure as time's travel.
I imagine it blank—
no thoughts, no words—
for I'm infinitely finite,
imperfect, just a creature—
not the Creator,
unable to know life's
forward motion.
Nor able would I be to see
the faces, the language of
gesture, the words spoken
to me or to others, and surely
the moment of my own death—
for these *whens* and *wheres*
exist only in the mind of God,
and he is keeping silent as to
their arrival.

Yet, this is *where* I'll be—
just in case you'll be
looking for me. *Whenever*
that may be.

What

The *what* of things seems always fixed
to *when* and *where* by a thin thread—about
to break under the strain of its importance.

For *what* must say with authority and sway
"We are gathered here today to . . ." and all
wait with goaded anticipation to become

aware of *what's* about to happen. We coped
with the knowledge of *when* and *where*—
though perhaps, we may labor under the

burden of knowing *what*, and deflect the
uncertain looks of others by simply saying
the rhetorical *"whatever!" When* and *where*

may have been injected with synthetic doses
of certainty—yet, *what* is often achieved by
faking it, or by a choleric beating of the manly

breast. The truth is this: the *what* may stare
us in the face, but usually we hardly know
what to do! And so, all too often we throw

up our hands and yell with utmost certainty,
"*What* a hell of a mess!"
The particular seems lost in the general.

But . . . maybe not. We shall see.

Who

1.

The first *who,* that creature of
human affairs—Adam, entered
the cosmos story at a disputed
when and a debatable *where*—
that successor of proto-men who
spilled their seminal fluid to no
avail, and lost their bid to rule the
earth—he is the *who* that became
the you and I that habitually ponders
the ultimate question: *who am I?*

2.

We were the ones *who* fled through
Eden's imagined gates, a fiery sword
lashing at our unguarded flanks.
We later huddled in the cold dew of
morning's early light, and asked of
each other: *who are you?*, and struck
a bargain there upon the ground, never
to remember paradise again.

Yet, we are the ones *who* carry on.

3.

We were the ones *who* watched
brother kill brother in a jealous fit,
and saw Cain flee to the city of the
damned with a mark upon his brow.
In it's streets brother still kills brother
without any reason other than the
rage within—of never remembering
paradise again.

Yet, we are the ones *who* carry on.

4.

We were the ones *who* watched Noah
build his boat *when* giants roamed
the earth in legend and in search of
fame. Yet our transgressions and
grief were piled high—though not
as high as the rain that came to wash
away any signs of paradise regained—
except a rainbow in the sky.

Yet, we are the ones *who* carry on.

5.

We were the ones *who* lost our first
language at Babel's tower, and fled
into a tangled history of curious
confusion, *who* had watched Nimrod
storm heaven's gates, *wasting* away
any right to human glory.

So now we storm each other's gates
to satisfy our appetites—never once
knowing *who* we are—existing just
outside the entrance to paradise.

6.
Yet, we are the children of Noah, *who*
carry on; from Shem to us we gather
in our breath and dream of home—
paradise being only a step away.

Why

Of all the analytical questions we ask
of life, the *when,* the *where,* the *what,*
and even the *who*—the *why* of things
strikes in us the greatest fear—often,
leaving us sensing an awesome chaos,
like wearing clashing colors and
disparate designs; helpless as we watch
storms coming—warm air meeting cold;
unconnected as *when* at a party, manic
meets depressive. Too big a *why*
becomes a huge collision of desperate
uncertainties, unanswerable questions,
a loss of confidence that the laws of
nature will continue working.

Think of the many *whys* you asked
as a child, never receiving an answer
you could understand. *Why* was an
innocent question, a quest, a flavor
you could try and easily put aside.
Why used to be fun, an exciting game,
a good way of exploring the world.
Why used to take us to places we'd
never been, ideas that stirred romance

in our soul.

Some*where*, some*how*,
why became a menacing word, a
mangled wreak, a crazy interjection
of "mild indignation, surprise or
impatience." And though we would
like answers, are afraid they won't
tell us *what* we want to know,
manipulating us into thinking *what*
we don't want to think, believing *what*
we don't want to believe, changing
what we don't want to change.

Now the *whys* seem a pesky nuisance,
a fly on life's salad or steak, a bother
in the senseless busyness of mindless
living.

Why became an orphan; even
philosophy & science skip the questions
before giving its answers; much religion
jumps straight to ritual without reward
to mind or heart, without challenge to
the status quo.

Of all the analytical questions we ask of life—
the *why* of things strikes in us the greatest
fear. And here we sit . . . afraid to ask the
all important *why*.

How

1.

And finally there's *How*—that runt of the
litter, that bastard child without the family
name, the almost abandoned Dickens'
kinsman—come to live as a foster child
among the particulars of the family tree—
left holding a familial bag full of general
when, where, what, who and *why.*

2.

She lives like a shadow for awhile, espying
the others while serving their needs,
returning at night to her dormer room,
and there by dim candlelight, *How* writes
it all down—that curious play between
siblings for the highest rank, the greatest
favor, the best advantage; for *How* is
ignored except for their wants, considered
helpless in her penury and lack of good
breeding.

3.

How must spend his time as a bootblack,
a coal shuttle, stableboy, a gardener who

trims bushes, pulls weeds and plants flowers.
His days are full of tasks that are hardly
noticed, but fully needed—duties hidden
from the eyes of others.

4.
The *Hows* labor in the great house or
extensive lawn while the *when, where,*
what, who and *why* lay about in an idle,
detached manner—having already played
their part in the grand scheme of things;
they've become careless in their adopted
aristocracy—forgetting that at the end,
How gets the credit for tidying things up,
making things right, while they are nearly
forgotten in the long string of getting life
from here to there.

Part Two

Life Beyond the Body

*[T]he term "dualism"... indicates
the belief that reality consists of
two distinct, absolute, and all inclusive
elements, most commonly identified as
matter and mind, or as [Robert] Frost
preferred, matter and spirit.*

—Peter J. Stanlis,
"Robert Frost,
Poet and Philosopher"

The Gift

Four small sea shells
in a crudely shaped,
unfired clay bowl—
a gift from a child
whose only design
is the satisfaction
of giving and
the pleasure of
the recipient.

Beauty is seen
best in the generosity
of love—a fragile
flower that can grow
in the humblest
of places—including
a crudely shaped,
unfired clay bowl,
filled with four
small sea shells.

At an Evening Art Class

The masters' ghosts moan low
in the midst of helpless prodigies,
whose knotted nerves tangle
in the fiber of the drawing paper.

And if the student delays in putting
down his lines, invisible fingers
may try to remove the pencil
from his or her unconfident hand.

Nevertheless, these ghosts must
content themselves with writing
their criticism on the back of clouds,
which are quickly blown away by

the winds of maturation.

Going on From Here

After the physical
intimacy of marriage,

a couple lay in bed,
pondering their

uncertainties . . .
much like relying

on the weather
in early spring.

They want to assemble
their feelings into

sensible meanings,
manageable categories.

The past is a flooded
river crossed . . . and

at present they gather
together their breaths,

for the future seems a
mountain to ascend

before the sun goes down.
Yet, at this moment . . .

just beyond the solace
of bodily union,

they weep freely in
each other's arms . . .

too weary to
go on from here.

Considering the Middle Distance

When Distance is Mainly a Thing of the Past

"But middle distance is best. Close up we see the
one leaf and the one tree, gorgeous but myopic; long
distance makes a momentary uniformity; best middle
distance offers tricks of focus . . . we take them in as a
leaf, as tree, and an expressionist's wild canvas."

—Donald Hall
"Seasons at Eagle Pond"

Like Hall writing about Autumn
leaf watching in New Hampshire,
I ponder the idea of viewing at
middle distance the many strange
particulars of life that may yet
emerge before me—perhaps, in
the few short years, months or
days left me in this world.

Yes . . . focusing *is* tricky;
the "long distance" is not there
(as Gertrude Stein might have
said in a different context);
the "momentary uniformity" a lie
against the inventory of human
sampling took so far.

The view of life's particulars
from "close up" can baffle
when the particulars no longer
seem relevant with the aging face
fit obliquely in my mirror—with
its curious lines and crevices, its
slackened and rebellious flesh.
The generation gap seems too wide
a jump to understand much of
the world's present mumbo-jumbo;
just using that phrase proves
how right I am.

Now, Mr. Hall assures me—I will
better fathom these present fancies
by looking at them from the middle,
where all particulars become a "wild
canvas"—while also, viewing each
one flash into view and out again
with the speed of cyberlight.

Perhaps, I should ignore the middle distance. If uproar and confusion were my delight—I could feast at their table all day long. However, that would *not* be the best. Better to view things from where I am.

Nocturne in Blue

To dream in certain nights
is to feel a particular grief
kept hid by day's blinding light.

For often in my dream-state
my wife's forever run away—
I, unable to follow in her flight.

What does it mean?, I ask.
Why does her shadow self
hide from me in these times?

Dreams follow life as our nights
follow day. Every thing comes
to roost in matters of the mind.

Necessarily, she sleeps in her
hospital bed, I, on my own—
a matter of forced separation.

Her dreams, you see, no longer
touch mine—that like our flesh,
that lies alone in nightly isolation.

—for Sal

Other People

When other people lay
their heads on their pillows,
do they remember anything

about me—the words I spoke,
the story I left behind,
the emotions I handed out

like invitations to a party?
Would they think it enjoyment
or a burden to endure?

Would they say goodnight
to this memory or shake
their minds loose of its dust?

When other people dream
do they dream about me—
perhaps as a super-hero or

just a ghost drifting in the gloom;
a champion on a grand mission,
or an uninteresting passer-by?

When other people rise
from their beds, do they think
how nice it would be to

encounter me in their waking
hours—or do they prefer a
discreet distance from the cast

of my shadow? Do other people
see me across a room and
wish I'd come near—sending

me a look that says this space
is meant for you—or do they hope
I'll turn away into my own private

musings? Do other people who
eat alone, wish for my company—
a kind blessing of presence

over their humble sandwich
or resolute salad—or do they
wish to remain in their own

sacred company, reveling in
the power of one, while thinking
of me as other people who

might think about them only as
other people? At best this seems a
perilous connection—leaving us all

lonely in a world of other people.

A Dispatch from the Ideological Front

"The figures on the chessboard were
still the passions and the jealousies and
superstitions and stupidities of man, and thus
positioned in regard to each other at any given
moment could be of interest only to the grim
faces who played the game . . ."

—Henry James
"The Princess Casamassima"

Black and white towers rise in cold dominance
over a weary horizon, the terrain surveyed
edged with the antagonisms of sophist partiality.
From these towers self-appointed kings mock
wisdom, sending out knights with poison swords

to search out their enemies—those who oppose
their doctrines and thirst for authority and rule.
Even now, their vendors of fear and ridicule
continue to leave calling cards on the doorsteps
of darkened castles, whose shadows hang over

the contested land like brooding storms.
The council of kings on either side of the great
divide are not conceding to loss of confidence.
Pieces on the Nietzschean front are reported
missing. Fumbling for answers, the caucuses

find their collective heads are empty, except for
the usual illusions and lies—the bishops having
voided corruption of the heart as a cause for
concern. Inside the castles, queens and rooks
walk through vacant rooms where no one

actually lives and no one actually is troubled.
Hopelessly obsessed with power and control,
they fold arms around hollow chests: gold plated
cages filled with unacknowledged greed like
birds too weary to fly above a sea of regret.

And in the gray mornings, pawns, born with
soiled fingers, are forsaken to a clotting
apathy. Weakness is their legacy; their rage
within grows. We are watching carefully.
No move is morally insignificant. Nothing

should be ignored. Every move is freighted
with taunt suspicion. Faithless men could die
of fright while waiting in silence for the game's
play to finally end.

Anger, Where Do You Hide

Where does Anger hide
when it doesn't desire to sing
its song of furious and mad defense.

What made you my concealed intimate,
you cursed and secret thing of mine
with your haughty power to consume.

How long did you need to hide
before you blossomed like a blemish
on the tip of my beggar's nose.

Did I call you from a hidden depth
which somehow I knew was there.
Oh Anger, do you dwell in a darkness

of your own that brings me to your door.
I could easily blame the world with its
pervasive heartache—or perhaps some

senseless judgment which seems to me
unfair. Heaven knows, oh Anger, I never
sought you or wished to hear your rants;

but there you were beside me—holding
down any better nature like a vicious clamp.
From your black heart answer if you can.

I know now your name has been my only
answer, and it hardly satisfies. Don't you
think it's high time we've had it out

before my questions become superfluous
and won't really matter to either you or me.

Independence Day Blues

Independence Day—
the birth of a nation;
American dreams are
being sung to the blues.

Picnics, picnics, our
fore-bearers celebrated
with picnics, music
from brass bands,
speeches, fireworks,
and plenty of dancing
into the night.

As a distracted nation
we celebrate with over-
indulgence. Over-
wrought, we can no
longer keep a handle
on our obsessions.
Over-stimulated, we
leap to conclusions.

Things are very busy
at the Crooked Lake
Ice-Cream Company.
Young waitresses—all
blond, rush back and
forth in breathless
synchronization to the
Independence Day Blues.

Prelude to a Nap

Having reached well past the age of
reason by what feels like centuries,
somewhere in the middle of my
afternoons, my physical and mental
energy flies the coop, and I am left
with an empty nest of a brain and
body, that cry out for rejuvenation
by way of the physiological state of
slumber.

Thus, I clear both my docket and my
sofa for the inevitable landing of my body
on the runway of possible REM sleep.

Quickly, I assume the correct position:
I lay on my right side, facing out, left arm
slung over my belly like a bandoleer, legs
stretched out to the full extent of my
resting height.
                    Then, according to protocol,
I cover my eyes with a greasy palm, or an
assortment of fingers, to keep the daylight
from hitting my eyelids—and possibly,
to keep my thoughts hidden from view—

those drifting thoughts and sudden insights
that often precede the coming of la la land,
possible dreams, and needed rest. A little
soft music in the background greases the skids
of my thinking and imagination, and I slowly
ride off toward distant places . . .

Wake me in twenty, please. Thank you.

Suddenly, I Miss . . .

my younger brother in late childhood, and I in
early adolescence—walking our dog, Squeaky,
a hound–terrier mix, through the streets of our
hometown. It is evening, mid-winter, dark, cold,
a light coating of snow on the sidewalk; perhaps
it is still snowing softly.

                    Behind the leash, we
follow small dog tracks and talk casually about
life as unseasoned boys working our way toward
manhood. We do not think of the tracks *we* have
left behind, and will not for a good many years.
A bit curious, we speculate on the lives played
out behind the lit windows of houses we pass.
What possible consciousness do they possess;
are they anything like ours?

                    In the chilled air
our breaths spread out before us—much like our
futures, as we head toward home and its warmth.

Thoughts on my Wife's Brain Report

*"Mind (Greek, "nous") The organ of mental
perception and apprehension, of conscious life,
of the consciousness preceding actions or
recognizing and judging them."*
> —from "The Complete Word
> Study Dictionary"

Be transformed by the renewing of your mind.
> —Romans 12:2

For fun she had taken an online test of her
brain's sharpness, and received this report:
*Things look pretty good, but there is
room for improvement.*

There was no end to the amusement
my daughter and I enjoyed at this vapid,
prepackaged cyber announcement—all at
my poor wife's fully thankless expense.

To me, what follows this come-on, no
doubt, is a nullification of mind in favor
of brain, the subservience of life as mere
stimulus for electro-chemical activity.

Why did the "test" chart my wife's "hardware"
and not also the sum of her experience?
Is not her "software" as vital as the matter
in her skull? As wonderful as the design

of the brain—*is* the activity of our minds.
For everything has its purpose under heaven.

Beelzebub Remembers Playing Pool with the Archangel Michael In the Hidden Places of the Previous Cosmos

"Then I saw three evil spirits that looked like frogs;
they came out of the mouth of the dragon, out of the mouth
of the beast and out of the mouth of the false prophet."
—the Apostle John,
Revelation 16:13

Here is where I lived for untold eons . . .
a fallen angel hovering over a green table—
a lonely galaxy stretching before my eyes
on which my clawed fingers danced like stars,
greedy arms extended like those of the Milky Way.

Silently, my cruel, twisted cue stick would slide,
shining, almost like the finger of God, (which,
stubbornly held me fast to my desperation), as
worlds collided beneath a smoking sun; hopefully,
finding their way into yawning black holes.

Yet, all too often I retreated back into darkness,
skirting the abyss, licking my wounds at another
loss to the archangel who wielded a nobler cue. I
would cry out in anger and emptiness at Jehovah,
who unfairly sent me away to finally lose it all.

A Sacramental Life

"Modern man cannot talk about
the object of his faith, only about the
faith itself . . . the value of faith depends
upon the object towards which the faith
is directed."

> —Francis A. Schaeffer,
> "The God Who is There"

Calculate the speed of light
and the life in the mirror
lives a millisecond behind
reality, leaving me just
another reflection in the
universe with all its stars
shining together over the
planet's cities reduced to
twinkling lights at thirty
thousand feet in different
places, at different times.

Is it any wonder I struggle
with this glimmer in my eyes,
trying to capture what the
Spirit sees, what he already

comprehends at the narrow
crossroad of my heart and
this world–all without the
benefit of sun or moon!

❖

Measure the speed of sound
and my ears are far behind
the voice that spoke creation,
the voice that now shouts
beyond the clouds, instructing
the angels, the voice that
wakens me at night, urging
me to intervene for a thing
unknown.

Yet, at the juncture of his
thoughts, and mine, I must
listen hard without the
advantage of wind *or* calm.
I must struggle against the
waves and particles that
crash through the first heaven
and onto this thrumming earth.

O, to hear what the Spirit
already hears, to know what
he already knows!

❖

Yet, something here in this
earthly life, something deep
within this profane wrapping,
causes me to search in the
dark places where his eyes
must be my eyes, his ears
my ears, in the confusion
of my own Babel. Thus, I
cry out with a muted voice:
Star and Wind–make me
human again.

Rita, *Child of Light*, and Her Window on the World

Rita's sensitive fingertips, trained by a resilient, aching love, search for the touch of archaic swirls in the flawed glass—tracing the pattern of all that has gone before: dreams spun out of sand, lost in the fury of a selfish, violent world adrift upon this lonely sphere of stone, a world that all too often resists true amity and the intercession of fervent tears. From her window on the world, Rita examines the heavy dust upon the outside sill. It often comes to lie deep after whirling in a strong storm of fruitless rationalization, a passing folly of false prophets whose fascinating promises never came to pass. The *Child of Light*, through experience, knows a stubborn resistance to reality intensifies all this; truth sifted to almost nothing by cultural delusions and calculated machinations. She knows this cannot lighten the souls of dispirited people, nor lead them to the paths they should walk. The *Child of Light* can taste the dust's sour smell upon her tongue without putting to her lips its bitter lie. Wiser than before her vigil commenced, she waits patiently for what is truly good and real; there will be no running after illusions. As evening comes, Rita tilts her head and looks in the mirror without seeing clearly all that lies between heaven and earth; yet, she knows in some better tomorrow, she will be a beautiful bride, prepared for her groom in all her splendor.

Distance

Like so many others, sometimes
I feel a terrible distance at the
3:00 AM hour; my awakened,
troubled mind takes me down a
stretch of dark, psychic highway—
unsure where it is going, but,
inevitably, knowing no good thing
is waiting for me there.

Do I only imagine the sound of
people talking in the street—their
voices too loud for the time of night?
It is as if there lay a great gulf
between them, and they cannot
understand the other because of the
dark. Then, when I hear the lonely
sound of footsteps fading beyond
my open window, I wonder if that
person has any idea of the distance
he or she has left behind, or the
distance intended in those footfalls?

When, finally, I reach to turn on a
light, hoping to dispel the room's
darkness, and my own sense of
alienation, the distance to the lamp's
switch seems a journey of many miles,
a desperate journey fraught with fear
of never arriving in a safe place, a
place close to the intimacy of my
mother's womb.

It is my belief . . .
we all are born to this world with a
terrifying distance burned into our eyes
at leaving the world of gestation and
the reassuring rhythm of our mother's
beating heart.
 Once here, we find ourselves
often living in the long divorce between
our desires and simple peace, splendid
contentment. It is like a spring through
winter cycle, with another April
bringing aspirations no nearer to fruition.
The reach of our longing, somehow
cannot bridge that terrible expanse.

And so, can there be a real end to this
distance that stands between us and
our imagined lives? Or as a searching
man once asked a very wise man,
"How can a man . . . enter his mother's
womb a second time to be born"!?

Christmas Morning, Creekside

A thrill of hope—the weary world
rejoices, for yonder breaks a new and
glorious morn!
>   —John S. Dwight, from
>   the Christmas carol
>   "O Holy Night"!

Water, once coursing in the earth,
no longer hides its consciousness
as it flows over the dropping level

of a creek bed. It speaks slowly
and quietly with a tinkling voice
and little sighs—but then grows

louder as it meets and then falls
in mini cascades over moss covered
rocks—clothed this morning in

Christmas greenery. This liquid
praise is no louder on this day than
any other, but seems to rise in the

still air and remain a second or two
longer than normal. It is a warm day
in late December—sunshine highlights

the bare limbs of the creek side trees,
the giant sycamore rising bone white.
Squirrel nests are huddled carefully

between the branches of other trees.
A few dandelions—a rare Christmas
flower—lie notably in the stubborn

grass of early winter, over which my
young hound runs and romps for joy.
Winter birds flit among naked shrubs

like holiday visitors arriving at the
door of family and friends.

❀

Despite all this, local groundhogs sleep
and refuse to awaken in their holes;
their attitude is balky—much like my

tired faith. My heart has grown cynical,
weary in a world that ritualizes solstice
more than it desires substance.

My faith does not flow as doggedly
as the waters of this stream, nor is my
devotion and praise like the rejoicing

of these humble, water-baptized rocks.
The countenance of my face is, perhaps,
not as bright as the smile of December

dandelions on this holy morning.
Defeat, or something similar, comes
to mind—but this thought is more

heedless than the thoughts of the
minnows that swim in the shadowy
pools of this creek. They know their

place in the world, while I feel absent.
Yet, I think of John Dwight's Christmas
lyrics that we sang on this day's eve, and

submit my faith for renewal in joy, peace,
hope, and love. For if a weary world's own
nature can rejoice on this glorious morn,

there is every good reason I can too.

To Name a Thing

For there is nothing hidden
that will not be disclosed, and
nothing concealed that will not
be known or brought out into the
light. Therefore, consider carefully
how you listen.
— Jesus, Luke: 8:17, 18

. . . everything exposed by
the light becomes visible, for it is
light that makes everything visible.
— The Apostle Paul,
Ephesians 5:13, 14

For better or worse,
to name a thing
is to bring it out of the
shadows of ignorance,
and unlock its secret—
casting light where things
might remain overlooked,
until . . . a certain thing

demands recognition with
angry, and sometimes,
violent protest. You see . . .
things are always waiting for
a name to be assigned and
spoken—acknowledged as
either good or evil, and given
the power to free or enslave.
It is simply . . .
       the nature of things.

First, however . . .
to name a thing is to
willingly ride the warm
thermals of the air—
unsure of when you might
fall from the heavens;
willingly swim within
the uncertain currents of
rivers and seas; or walk
the untrod paths of earth—
yes . . . to readily travel
to a thing's destination,
no matter its intention,
and willingly share any
responsibility for its
      existence.

Further, remember this . . .
In any deliberation to
name a thing, you *must*

first encounter, endure,
and overcome a child's
fear; perhaps, the rage
and craze of adolescence;
even the subtle corruptions
of so-called maturity, and
possibly, the indignation
of old age.

      For only through
these and grace will you
gain the mastery to rightly
name a thing. Best consider
all this before taking on one
of the most important tasks
in the world.

Dancers

The dilemma is that we no
longer know what it means to be
human.

—James Emery White,
"Serious Times"

We seem to live like dancers
without partners in a world
devoid of music and rhythm.
We go from one dance to
another—looking for the
perfect song, the perfect
moment when the dance
has meaning.

For argument's sake . . .
consider the gypsy-like
dancers—the hot tempered
offspring of angry fathers,
and steely mothers,
who shake the scented dust
of seduction from cake-mix
bodies—to kindle attraction

and find some satisfaction
in another lonely night—
only to swallow up the life
of another, just to feel alive
for a time. Or . . . just as often
swallowed up themselves in the
emptiness of another.

Don't fool yourself . . .
despite fantasy's colored light,
these dancers and others are
as empty and distant as passing
dreams, as far away as the stars
that dance in the night sky.
Get real . . . these dancers
are nothing more than
neon signs that blink on . . .
and then off.

Oh, voyager, think not tonight
of their genitals and yours,
your desire and theirs, your
lust and theirs—trading one
illusion for another, colliding
in some imagined dance of life.

Better to dance with those stars
of the night; at least their fire is
real, their heat true, their light
enduring, their distance . . .
closer than you would think.

And, in case you didn't know—
add more energy to life's hopes
than any intermittent flashes
of colored light and scented dust.

Go on . . . shine like a star in a
dark night. Who knows . . .
someone might ask you to dance.

In God's Room

The fool says in his heart,
There is no God.

—Psalm 14:1

Bored with sifting through back
copies of intellectual and scientific
journals, a clever man wandered
down the hallway to where it was
rumored that God had rented a
room on a weekly basis. The man
chuckled to himself: apparently,
God was not certain how long he
would remain in the city, or for
that matter—in the world.

Talk about was that God stayed
aloof, spending time in his room,
doing heaven-only-knows-what.
Some thought they saw him
standing in the window, staring
out through a filmy veil. It was
remembered by some that it
was said—to see God's face

was to die. And so, the man had
checked his journals: no scholar
had confirmed this; no PhD
candidate had launched a thorough
study and written a dissertation;
no scientific papers recorded such
research. Many reported that busy
acting strangers in similar garb
entered and left the building
on a regular basis. Others thought
they heard knocking on God's door
at all hours of the day and night.
The man thought perhaps all this
was just people's imagination;
he had not seen nor heard any
of this. Sloughing it off, the man
remembered what a wise man
named Friday once said: "Give us
the facts . . . just the facts."
He was not sure in what journal
he read this; yet, he was sure
of its wisdom.

Stopping at what he thought was
the door of God's room, the man
considered knocking and introducing
himself; he would investigate and
put an end to all these rumors.

However, he hesitated and backed
away, listening for voices rising
and falling in the private space beyond.
Nothing. Yet, he sensed someone there—
hidden from view, secreted from sound,
and probably annoyed by curious
attempts upon his time. Then . . . he
heard a voice call out—not loud or
shouting—but quiet and clearly coming
through the door: *Come in, I've been
waiting for you. You are right on time.*

Covington Square

The poet Crowley said to us: "Are any
of us able to defend ourselves against
ourselves as we live within our social
lives? How can we say our lives are
without, at least, a hint of pretense,
or prejudice against the truth that lays
us bare before the world"? It was then
he told us of his visit to Covington
Square, that place in Crowley's words:
"part of the city-scape, that anthill
gathering by day, the place of social
worship," where he knew the structure
gave some relevance to an obviously
pretend importance.

We sat in our overstuffed chairs, fitted
with leather, the air filled with the smoke
of pipes and fat cigars, the brandy in our
glasses—a red glow shining in the light
of the evening's fire. Within the comfort
of our club, we listened to our poet friend
tell of his latest adventure.

Though well hidden behind self-satisfied
smirks and cynical smiles, we felt disturbed
at his descriptions of "paper doll clothes" and
"drag queen wigs." The poet told us of the
strange people who entered Covington Square
by fall of night. Where propriety reigns by day,
came tales of dissipation, envy, seduction,
madness and uncontrolled liberty in the night.
Crowley spoke of a spirit, an atmosphere unlike
that of daylight hours in the park, where mothers
or nannies converse with each other over baby
carriages, while older children play; where
gentlemen stroll alone or with a companion
on the paths running among the trees. How
strange I thought, I have been to Covington
Square . . . but, only by day. In covert glances,
with silent lifts of brow, and wry grins, we
asked of each other:

Why does Crowley talk of such things?
We know him to be a poet, and a poet lives
on the edge of polite society. Yet, we allow
him some grace, for he is a 'high-strung'
artist, a good fellow all around if a bit odd
at times. Let us humor him for our own
amusement.

Yet, an ill-at-ease was in the room, a sense
that Crowley had suddenly come upon some
deeply hidden reality, while stumbling around
in his dreamy, poetic world. We knew ourselves

as men of importance, of business and weighty
affairs, men of integrity and moral strength,
with the weight of the masses on our shoulders.
Crowley knew us well as . . . irreplaceable men!

Who of such high regard would care to know
of such goings on in public squares? Such
things would surely offend a gentleman's social
sensitivities. Surely, Crowley's tale cannot be
true. Did he intend to put this awful scene in
his verses, hoping to stir the imaginations of
the less refined, the less educated? Nervous
laughter emptied the room, leaving behind
noxious smoke and half-drained glasses;
his narrative unsettled us so we departed to
our own apartments to ponder this disturbing
story. I myself was strangely caught up in his
tale of Covington Square, and was much
induced to visit the place—despite my
apprehension of such a delirious scene.

As the evening crouched like a stalking beast
outside Covington's iron fence—I felt within
me a strange expectancy—finding myself
dreading that Crowley's tale might be a
fabrication, a hoax played upon the minds of
his contented friends; I was afraid I would
not look upon the transformation of the square.
And yet . . . they came in ones and twos—
those revelers who filled the square at night,
wearing masks and costumes of rare

appearance—all dancing and swirling in a
savage display of teeming life.

Yet, I noticed they neither touched nor spoke
with words to each other—only gesturing with
unknown signs and symbols that escaped
without genuine comprehension. Then the
masks came off and the most horrible faces
of men appeared—wretched, pale, ghostly,
alive but hardly so; seemingly vacuous men.
However, the worst is yet to be told.

Though vastly abased in appearance, these
same men had sat around that early evening's
fire with me—enveloped in smoke and
swaddled in drink. We had deemed Crowley's
tale an insane dream—one in which its telling
we had hoped to escape; to think, I purposely
entered into such a madness! I could not take
this awful scene and fled to the comfort of my
familiar rooms, where brandy gave no solace
to my agitated mind, nor my many books—
a sufficient answer, an explanation for the
specters I saw in the unkind light of the square.

Continuing in my disturbance, I went to my
toilet to refresh myself—only to find my
reflection in the mirror as I saw the others
in the square. I too was vastly disfigured and
sunken within. How could this apparition appear
before me!? The answer was all too clear: I too

must be most pitiful among the mass of these important men!

Love and Creation Suite

That Which Existed Before Time and Space

Genesis 1 & 2; Isaiah 45:18; Rom. 8:19-21

That which existed before time and
memory, God infused in the tiny seed
of the cosmos with such force as to

cause it to explode —the seed being
unable to contain the energy, matter *and*
the ageless infusion of transcendent love

held within its infinitesimal dimensions.
The seed expanded at an incredulous rate
throughout a void we can only imagine.

And what came forth through millennia
was declared good in holy writ—long before
Adam forsook his right of holy rule. Then,

came cosmic war within creation—that evil
would destroy its beauty, its purpose to glorify
God and provide for the world's needs. Yet,

even now, the Creator's essence—infused
within creation's secret places—resists the
tyranny, desiring only that men steward in

loving relation with God and all that awaits.

That Which Holds All Things Together

Psalm 33:4-6; 1John 4:16; Colossians 1:15-17

God reveals himself in creation, for the very core
of the earth is fused together with agape' love—
the structure of nature held in concert with the Son's

righteousness at its quantum level—the uncreated
creating the fabric of space and time, the seen and
and the unseen, material and mystery blended deep

in the preexisting, always existing, primordial soup
of divine love and holy will.

That Which Offers the Good of Creation

1 Timothy 4:4-6

Through the testimony of the Logos, and the
experience of divinity's essence, we come to
know that in creation's efficiency, all things

were forged in the holy fire of agape' love—
once made of heavenly quality and character—
worthy of every man's use and praise. For

the emphatic "good" of God's sacred opinion
embraces and sets apart all material things—
seen and unseen, and are now offered as holy

gifts to us who live under the shadow of the
Almighty's outstretched arm. Amen and amen.

Still Life at Forty-Something

Five voices, filled with laughter, journey
across the gulf of a table top like sailing
ships carrying cargoes of words and wit.
Although the one middle-age man knows
there is a distance of time between himself
and a just-graduated college miss, he
wonders if the space of a table top might
be the only gulf. And so, he watches from
his shore for the signal in her eye—telling
him she has received his latest shipment.

He listens as she talks of the antics of her
recent life, her careless manner, trying to
stand out in the university crowd around
her. He notices her eyes shining like
colorful hot-air balloons in a blue sky.
They draw him helplessly into her world,
and he wishes, for a moment, to have
been a part of her indiscretion. Yet, he

realizes his vulnerability, and tries to
retreat to a far corner of his mind. But
he knows he's quite disarmed; it's true—
his heart's been cut by the curved blade
of her smile.

Despite himself, he's been ridiculous,
trying to speak her language with its
unrelieved playfulness. But it's no good,
she's taken his measure with friendly, but
mischievous banter, and all he can do is
find her velvet beating disconcerting.

Feeling wounded—but not hurt, he knows
he's been bound, left helpless, thrown
about by strange forces. He hopes to come
away only tenderly bruised and slightly
ashamed. A man at forty-something can
play the fool at particular times in his life.

On Memory

Memory has its own mechanics.
When an experience is complete,
and time has drained from its
essence, the reflections left behind
are carefully picked up by mind
machines and put into little boxes—
each marked with appropriate
names, emotions and places,

then stored away in dark closets
filled with images kept from fading
in the brilliant light of another day—
until the door is opened in the late
hours of a sleepless night by a
foraging heart, only to find them
all together alien.

On Wishes Being Horses and Beggars Allowed to Ride

Social arrangements live on
in the individual, buried in the mind
below the level of consciousness.
                    —Christopher Lasch

Waking from a myth of unceasing
progress, I see the busy brains of
corporate CEO's, technocrats,
politicians, and generals in a state
of suspension; drool from gaping
mouths shimmer on a map of a
battered & besieged world.
The human weakness for things,
influence, and power is no longer
manipulated by the schemes of
market puppeteers.

I see shaded benches where
unhurried, unwired people read
books made of paper, tell parables
to one another, maybe sing songs,
or pray to a God—if not fully
understood, at least is somewhat

known. Others write letters to
friends with a pen, or look forward
to eye to eye discourse around ideas
that matter to the soul, that exhorts
the spirit; no longer does gossip
and vitriol rule the patterns of
our speech.

The workplace is strangely calm;
labor goes on sans a "sense of inner
emptiness," that feeling of a "weak
sense of self." The power to make
man a machine has disintegrated;
the soul of man survives.

Family kitchens and dining rooms
are occupied with people eating
meals together. Hosts and guests
enjoy the ritual of chatter over
their food while hearing the rhythm
of life and beholding the color of
one another's dreams. Here wide-
eyed children within the safety-net
of parental love listen to stories
that make them wise as well as
strong against monsters both real
and imagined.

The body is no longer worshiped;
transformation aims at higher
things. Anger fades in the time

it takes for renewed minds to hear
the reasoning of our bettered selves.
Psychology has become the newest
alchemy; most have turned to
seeking wisdom rather than trying
to turn excuses into gold. Thus,
no longer is the pathological
another version of normal.

I see schools and universities
where disinterested teachers,
philosophers, and professors,
investigate the meaning of
life, while others pass on the
knowledge gained through the
observation of reality—where
the love of learning outweighs
desire for ideological mastery.

I see religions that are more
interested in knowing God
than knowing control, personal
gain or political power. The

world of arts and letters is no longer
severed from the Midwest farmer,
the Wyoming cowboy, or the
average suburban couple, by the
cacophony of gratuitous, personal
rebellion against social restraint,
or the constant buzz of what's
"relevant" in the minds of the critics.

Love and romance is no longer a battleground where the lonely or selfish compete for the greatest self-gratification, where sexual conquests are not noted with shiny medals of hedonism and self-promotion. In the clear light of day we can see that love goes well beyond the boundaries of sensual utopia, that romance is more than bodice bursting, or another form of human self-actualization. Instead, lovers live for the giving of themselves.

In this fantasy in black and white, life has become much like a homemade parade. We have nothing in our hands except our fertile imaginations. We carry no placards. We chant no ridiculous slogans. Our genuine self-hood and concern for others is visible for all to see.

Part Three

Life of Poets and Poetry

*We are thus indelibly marked by
the poems we read, and the more
poems we read the deeper is our
knowledge of the world . . . The poem is
the device through which the ordinary
world is seen in a new way—
engaging, compelling, even beautiful.*

—Ted Kooser,
"The Poetry Home Repair Manual"

The Birth of Poetry

No one can experimentally
validate or rule out conjectures that
apply beyond the horizon.
 — Lisa Randall, physicist,
  "Dark Matter and the Dinosaurs"

I figure it started like the Big Bang—
hot, expansive, and without structure,
words flying out on a flat surface
with tremendous energy—cooling
down into syntax—forming lines
and stanzas like particles on a white
background of inventive radiation.

Even now, dark matter clusters in
creative brains, giving future life
to galaxies of poetic constellations—
writers and readers filling the literary
cosmos like abundant dark energy.

A Translucent Language

The ideal of lyric poetry . . .
is to be this passive, flawless medium
for the deeper consciousness of things,
the mysterious voice of that mystery
which lies about us . . .
      —Arthur Symons, quoted in
      "The History of Modern Poetry"
      by Dr. David Perkins

Today, reading in a house
empty of others—its silence
so real, so electric, it buzzed

in my head—poems floated
through the room, holding up
the odd shape of people, places,

and events before the softness
of a full moon, turning in circles
the curious states of mind,

energy and ambition, until all
human contradictions made sense.
Words like tanks of air enabled me

to dive to the bottom of dark rivers,
dodging rocks, slipping through
slime, where all the mysteries of the

world reside—silvery interpretations
hiding in the shadows like small fish
in the murky dullness of our souls.

A feathery breath, lodged between
pages, urged me to watch the snow
fly in circles around my kitchen

window, and realize—as seen through
a translucent language—my life has
come to this point, and I am not alone.

Who Writes Poetry Anyway?

Considering the ways in which so
many of us waste our time, what would be
wrong with a world in which everybody
were writing poems?
                              —Ted Kooser,
              "The Poetry Home Repair Manual"

Sitting in my car at a busy
intersection, I note a late
middle-aged man with a
slightly expanded body,
and short white beard
astride a big Harley bike.

He wears the usual garb:
chunky black boots,
leather vest with the
Harley logo on the back,
and a radically printed t-shirt
atop the essential faded jeans.

Oh, and sans helmet. I muse:
does this biker write poetry?

Does he even read poetry?
Does he know what poetry is?
Does he care what poetry is?

It may be unfair of me to think
the answer to all these questions
is no, negative, an *absolute* zero.
He could be composing a sonnet
in his head as he sits, throttling
in neutral, waiting to turn against
oncoming traffic. He could be
debating with himself over the
"best words in the best order."

This biker may be on his way
to his favorite café, where he'll
order a cappuccino, get out an
expensive notebook and pen, and
begin drafting dynamic free verse—
similes, symbols, and metaphors
flashing like the chrome pipes
on his big old, masterful Harley.
He roars past me in a biker's blast
of acceleration; most likely in a

hurry to get to a poetry reading
where he'll share his newest work
with the motorcycle gang that
just ran the last critic out of town.

The Past is Full of Dead Poets

The successful poem is a microcosm
of this other world and a microcosm of the
poet . . . it is a microcosm of the time and
society in which it was written.

> — Stephen Dobyns,
> "Best Words, Best Order"

It's perhaps a photo taken by
Flossie Williams: the poets of
Others: A Magazine of New Verse
stand or crouch in two neat rows on
Dr. Williams' Rutherford, NJ lawn,
early spring, 1916—modern poets,
artists, and fellow brothers of bohemia—
decked out in shapeless suits, hands
jammed in coat pockets or wrapped
tight in folded arms, elbows steadied
on bended knee.

The poets are Skip Cannell,
Alfred Kreymborg, Bill Williams,
Alanson Hartpence, Pitts Sanborn,
Walter Arensberg, and Maxwell
Bodenheim. Looming is the absence
of Mina Loy—first poet published in
Others, and Miss Moore with her jug
of carrot juice and loaf of whole wheat
bread. Did the boys in masculine pride
wait for this particular day to have
their picture taken? We think not . . .
Wallace Stevens was off somewhere
making money for Hartford Life &
Casualty.

The Swiss painter, Jean Crotti,
the French artist of *Nude Descending
a Staircase* fame—Marcel Duchamp,
and American artist, Man Ray—later
an expatriate—have come to bind ties
with these American men of verse,
and, no doubt, with Walter Arensberg,
sometime poet, patron, and collector
of the arts.

Modern poetry is at an exciting start.

Not all stare resolutely into the lens
on this sunny April day in 1916:
Duchamp has put his arm through
the crook of Arensberg's elbow
in a display of rife French solidarity
with these artful, cutting edge men.
He looks away from the camera,
his mind, possibly on another
"ready-made," or a game of chess.
Bill Williams—bound for later literary
influence and fame, holds tight a
squirming black cat; either it doesn't
quite appreciate modern art, or being
held up involuntarily before a camera
lens. Kreymborg—chess player, poet,
playwright, puppeteer, and *Others*
editor, with hat set at a jaunty angle,
stares at Williams' feline friend—
perhaps thinking he protests too much.
Hartpence, author of *The Poisoned Lake*
and Cannell, *imagist* and admirer of
Old Testament poetry, are crouching at
each end of the front row like bookends.
Both seem caught off guard at the shutter's
opening, perhaps thinking the squirming cat
an omen of the eventual collapse of this
modern *Magazine of New Verse?*

A slouching Max Bodenheim with floppy
hair—parted in the middle—is set apart
to the far right; the paper he holds is
conceivably too weighty with cogent
words. His future will be a slow slide
into personal and literary desolation:
Max will meet with a violent death
in a Greenwich Village flophouse in '54.

A tall and stately Pitts Sanborn prefers
to put his manuscript in a jacket pocket,
placing his arms behind his back
like a general reviewing his troops.
His bespeckled eyes look off to some
notoriety as a music critic, novelist . . .
and death by heart failure at 61.

It's a New Jersey day in April, 1916;
all are dead poets bereft of knowing.

The Elements of Poetry

Recent poets . . . have opted
for a looser, rangier, more naturally
discursive mode for their poems, and
usually they have set the core controlling
device deep inside the work.
                    —Jack Myers,
        "The Portable Poetry Workshop"

Found: a slip of paper in a
second hand anthology—
English 329
Elements of Poetry.

The elements are in *bold* type—
exerting themselves on the
consciousness of the student,
pushing intimate relationship,
almost forcing themselves on the
innocence of the would-be artist.
However, the categories
do not tell what they should;
their meanings are meant for
acolytes, for fellow travelers only.

I would revise as thus:

Word Choice: Whatever
your head, heart, muse, or
desperation would have you use.

Imagery: What screams the
loudest in your ears, blinds
your optic nerve, burns
your nose, and cuts your
fingers to the bone.

Figures of Speech: Say it in
words likened to the curves
and voice of the flesh.

Style: Disregard the house
of fashion; wear it proudly.

Form: Drop it from a bridge;
see what happens.

Theme/Idea: Whatever, it's poetry.

Portrait of an Online Poet

We make poetry out of our conflicts,
our warring opposites . . . and we may not
know we do.

      —Donald Hall,
    "Breakfast Served Anytime All Day"

She wore poems around her neck like amulets
to ward off the virtual dangers of cyberspace,

singing colorful songs, stringing them like nets
across the horizon to stop the sun from slipping

into the earth and out of sight. She hoped to lay
gentle words like brocade over the unpleasant

roughness of the human condition I revealed in
a poem. Wanting to conceal its crueler surface,

she composed exotic music with a new-age psyche,
trying to fill the empty spaces that she felt others

had left behind in their haste to show their stuff
to the online poetry world. All the while, she played

games of wit with abandon, tossing ribbons of her
amused subconscious like confetti onto the steady

parade of poetics that passed like poorly designed floats
across her safely guarded computer with its filtered screen.

—for Anastasia (2005)

All Poems Before the Broken Branch
Had Lost Their Light

and like James Wright I lay
aside a book of bad poetry.
God knows I've written my
share—but in my case
familiarity does not breed
contempt—only frustration.

According to some reports
James Wright was a complex
man—out on a limb, waiting
for the branch to break.
God knows, aren't we all. He
wrote some beautiful poems—
this man who slept alone in
visited farmhouses and
roamed Minnesota pastures
in search of solace.

Yet he leaves me wanting to
know what *he* came to know
while lying in William Duffy's
hammock on a sunny day in
the country; I'm unsure how
he encountered the world—
with resolution *or* regret?

Whatever the answer, my lie-
down is a sleepless four AM
sofa with a stained ceiling
overhead and a wife tossing
covers just above. However,
I have not yet wasted my life.

An Old Curmudgeon's Poemosophy

If it ain't a pleasure, it ain't a poem.
                    —William Carlos Williams

I could be in trouble for
saying this in the present
land of poetry . . .
the parents of my own poems
are the generation after
my father's, the so-called
"Silent Generation," now
dead or grown very old . . .
those who made their way
out of the shadows of 1940's
New Criticism, those still read
by the admirers of early
postmodern poetry,
long before post-postmodern
experimental verse became a
flurry of words across the page,
spilled out without syntax, metaphor,
similes, rhythm, music, and
worst of all . . . meaning. Well,
perhaps their meanings are not
meant for me. So be it.

On what Prof Perkins called in
The History of Modern Poetry
the "postwar period" of
American poetry, I cut my
poetic teeth, reading Ginsberg,
Ferlinghetti, Koch, Creeley,
Field, Kooser, James Wright,
Merrill, Bukowski, Cohen,
and later poems by Bishop,
Stafford, Lowell, Berryman,
and W.C. Williams.
Even now I read Hall, Bly,
Pastan, Levertov, Oliver,
Kenyon, Kumin, Stroud, Hass,
Charles Wright, Ignatow,
Justice, Levine, and other
poets of this *not so* silent
generation. I realize, this list
could bore the uninitiated.

Fellow poets of the present scene:
please forgive an aging and,

perhaps, reactionary man of letters;
I seldom recognize the names
of poets that fill the newer
anthologies, journals and websites.
Most are strangers to my reading
habits, for I mostly live in the old
neighborhood of used poetry books;
bygone names on their well-worn

covers visit me while I drink my
morning coffee with my young
hound on the sofa next to me.
She offers no opinion of my tastes.
Even in our short time together
she has learned not to argue
with a curmudgeon poetry lover,
or she might not get that first
dog biscuit of the day.

A Difficult (if Not a Dangerous) Art

We seem trapped between
a tediously mechanical view of
poems and an unjustifiably
shamanistic view of poetry
itself . . . it's easy to feel that
your response to the art is
somehow wrong . . .
> — David Orr,
> "Beautiful & Pointless"

Let's be real for a moment . . .
it's likely a poem never
changed the world,
nor many people
for that matter—
if *that* is even possible
through the mere
words of fellow humans.

Has it been documented
that poetry has prevented
armed men from
killing each other?
I wish it could.
It would seem, Mars—
that capricious
god of war—
pays little mind
to the protests of
aggrieved artists.
I wish he did . . . but,
he seems quite absorbed
with his one passion.

I could be wrong . . .
Poetry has seldom
convinced weary men
of their worth—
or conversely,
convicted the hubris
that inflates minds
to the size of
cumulus clouds,
their aspirations equal
to the density of such
an airy substance,
and full of the same
turbulence.

As wonderful as some are,
poems barely scratch
the surface of
the convolutions
humans live by
most of the time.
Yet, we keep trying.

We read how
critics and erudite
composers of verse
often proclaim—
poetry reveals *truth*,
or at least a certain
idea of *truth*, a sense
that certain ideas
and values do matter.
At the least it conveys
the idea that familiarity
matters to most people
in this world . . .
and that it prevails
most of the time.

Perhaps . . .
but does this idea
of *truth* wait
outside the doors
of cloistered rooms
for an invitation
from the poet
to enter and reveal
itself on empty paper?

I think not.

It is easy to see—
poetry can be
a difficult—if not
a dangerous art,
best practiced
in the revealing
light of heaven,
and while walking
this earth as a witness
to what really is.

Wandering Poems

This much is certainly true:
the free verse poem, when finished,
must 'feel' like a poem—it must be
an intended and effective presentation.
                    —Mary Oliver,
                "A Poetry Handbook"

Sometimes my poems are like
stray prose dogs who wander
through poetic neighborhoods
in search of cast-off rhythms,
music, the perfect line.

If you happen to see one—
sniffing at the scent of some
stale meter, point it in the
direction of the nearest
rejection slip—

                    and yell *git!*

Oscar and the French Photo

In the gloom of early morning, light
just illuminates Oscar, my cantankerous
striped tiger cat, who yowls in my
window at nothing—for nothing moves
in the yard or beyond at this time of day.
He wants me to know it's time to awake
and meet the coming day. He is a feline
poet of protest, a bard of bad behavior,
a versifier of the tenacious, whose poems
are quite in line with performance art, and
the best of poetry slams.

Annoyed with my unresponsiveness,
he moves to a framed photograph
near my bed, paws at its base, and
pulls it nearly forty-five degrees
toward horizontal, letting it fall back
to the wall with a clatter—all to
rouse me from my lazy slumber; not
just once, but repeatedly he tries this ploy.
Without forethought I yell, "knock it off,"
right away realizing he cannot decipher
this from the Gettysburg Address; yet,
I feel foolish for telling him to do what
I don't want him to do . . .

Then, with an absorbed and determined look, Oscar stares into this nighttime picture of the lit-up *Restaurant La Mere Catherine* on the *Place du Tertre* in Paris, France. Perhaps, Oscar notices this scene differs from his regular view through the bedroom window; here, he sees patrons sitting at their tables in the red hue of a Parisian night. But what he doesn't know, he's looking upon this strange world as a long exposure of trapped time and place. Yowling at the photo gets no result, so he rattles the frame against the wall—in an effort to get these forever stilled people moving again. It should also be said: he sees himself as an unwavering critic of any current scene.

Intimate Literary Moments

Allow me to show you exhibits of
intimate literary moments from my
bookshelves:

A.
Sometime in 1893 Patience B. Dingee
received, "with regards of E. H.,"
Thoughts by the Way, a handsome book
of self-published religious and inspirational
poems by Eliza Heaton, printed 1891 in
Poughkeepsie, NY by A.V. Haight—bought
by myself years ago at a yard sale in upstate
New York. It looks its age at almost a hundred
and thirty years—oftentimes, lovingly held,
and lovingly read.

B.
Paul wrote a short note to Pat in the flyleaf
of *The Collected Poems of Howard Nemerov*
(1981 edition)—a gift of parting to a colleague
of many years. Paul tells Pat, Nemerov is his
"favorite poet," claiming him "profound,
humorous, and irreverent." He hopes

Nemerov's poems will provide his friend
with "many warm thoughts." The years old
paperback appears in pristine condition—
not much handled, nor ofttimes read.
I now own this once graciously given book.

C.
Art A. received a signed copy of Richard
Jones' *The Blessing* on May 20, 2000. I now
own Jones' signature and his once *New and
Selected Poems,* bought from *Bargain Books.*

D.
2019, a New Hampshire poet wrote on
the title page of a poetry book: "for my
beloved pal, Steve, with admiration and
affection." Steve was very careful not to
bend the cover or crease a page. Looks
like it just arrived from the publisher's
stock.

❖

How many poetry books have been given
as gifts—signed by friends with wonderful
intention—others autographed by yearning,
thankful poets who wondered if anyone will
care they spent time writing these precious
poems. But, then . . . hardly read—sold to
used bookstores for pennies, or tossed in
Goodwill bins—later pulled off either packed

or cyber shelves, perhaps sloppy piles by
strangers like me?

         It's here among these labors
I wander and browse among such castoffs,
quietly opening to flyleaf or title page,
suddenly sensing I've opened a closed door
and walked in uninvited, unannounced, and
awkward at coming upon the occasion of
private, almost intimate moments when
presenter or artist opened their lives to
another with ink and thoughtful words, and,
perhaps, their cherished hopes.

Should I feel like a voyeur, or an archaeologist
whose stumbled upon a buried possession
that tells us something of the literary world?

Time Out of Mind & Personal Salvation

Haunted anew by Auden's anxiety
I laid low in my cave with a wife
and soon two kids—scrawling
poems of angst—angry about the
notional darkness just outside my door:

So as the golden days
pass into the blackness we crave,
we leave bits of ourselves on
bar-tops and half empty glasses
of good intentions we never
finished or even tried. It comes
so hard–the waiting for the last
chance to redeem our lives.

Many fine surveyors of verse
could not keep my mind from
slipping into a darkness that now
engulfed my cave—nearly wasting
all that I was or ever hoped to be.
As Carter's "malaise" overtook a
weary nation, I wrote a few plaintiff
lines from the hospital mental ward:

The bones of my body—
even to my skull, are
hollow as empty cartons.

The poets failed to join me in my
bewildered state. Neither Crane,
Plath, nor Sexton hunkered with
me in a smoke-burdened lounge
filled with haggard spirits, while
we waited on pills or a dose of
electric shock. Yet, I must confess,
I didn't invite them to come. Hiding
from my psyche's hollow pain, I
cowered with a cheap paperback
below the dark clouds that hung
just inches above my bed. Carter
didn't send a get-well card.

Yet, like the Earth, the heart turns
in an orbit. From solstice to solstice,
it travels around the things we fear
unto the One who loves—while, from
equinox to equinox, it journeys

from empty longing to what a heart
truly needs. So, I traveled through
the night on Dylan's *Slow Train*
Coming, and wakened to Reagan's
"Morning in America." Yet, the
light didn't come from the White
House, nor from poetry shelves in

cluttered bookshops, but out of
the darkness slowly left behind—
revealing a path ahead to greener
pastures, stiller waters. I returned
to my cave in submission and
received a hidden strength.
Seeking the heavens, I gained earth's
blessings. Embracing the "Ground
of Being," I found my soul and spirit
renewed.

(1979 – 1981)

Notes

❧ *"When."* Epignosis (pronounced e-pē'-gnō-sēs) is a Greek word meaning **precise and correct knowledge**.

❧ *"When."* "I will know as I am known." 1 Corinthians 13:12.

❧ *"Rita, Child of Light . . ."* Rita represents the contemporary Church and its role as watchman, encourager, and giver of light through the preaching of the Gospel of Jesus Christ to a lost, and broken world. The name "Rita" means "Child of Light." Rita was also my mother's name.

❧ *"Distance."* "How can a man . . . enter his mother's womb a second time to be born"!? John 3:4.

❧ *"Covington Square."* This poem is based on a short poem by a poet friend (the "Crowley" mentioned in the opening verses). With his permission and encouragement I build upon on his poem about Covington Square in my own narrative way. Many thanks to my poet friend for the inspiration.

❧ *"A Translucent Language."* Arthur Symons was a leading British "Symbolist" poet of the 1890's.

NOTES

↬ *"Portrait of an Online Poet."* It should be noted that there was never any personal animosity between myself and the poet known as "Anastasia." This poem merely reflects my amusement over the personality and world-view differences between two poets. If I remember right, "Anastasia" wrote some beautiful poems.

↬ *"An Old Curmudgeon's Personal Poemosophy."* "Prof Perkins" is David Perkins, who was a professor of English and American Literature at Harvard University. Perkins wrote a two volume, "History of Modern Poetry," (Harvard University Press) which covered marvelously both English and American poetry in the years from 1890 until about 1980. This poem was written with a bit of "tongue in cheek," though it does represent my view of certain contemporary poetry.

↬ *"Time Out of Mind & Personal Salvation."* "Auden's anxiety" refers to "The Age of Anxiety: A Baroque Eclogue" (1947), a long poem in six parts by W. H. Auden. "The poem deals with man's quest to find substance and identity in a shifting and increasingly industrialized world." (Wikipedia). "Carter's malaise" refers to President Jimmy Carter's speech in which he referred to what he saw at the time as an overall spiritual depression most Americans felt during a time of high economic inflation, and the aftereffects of the exhausting experience of the "Watergate" scandal, and its long political drama played out on national television. I mention being in my "cave." This thought comes from an essay by Gerald Stern, who as a poet calls himself a cave dweller.